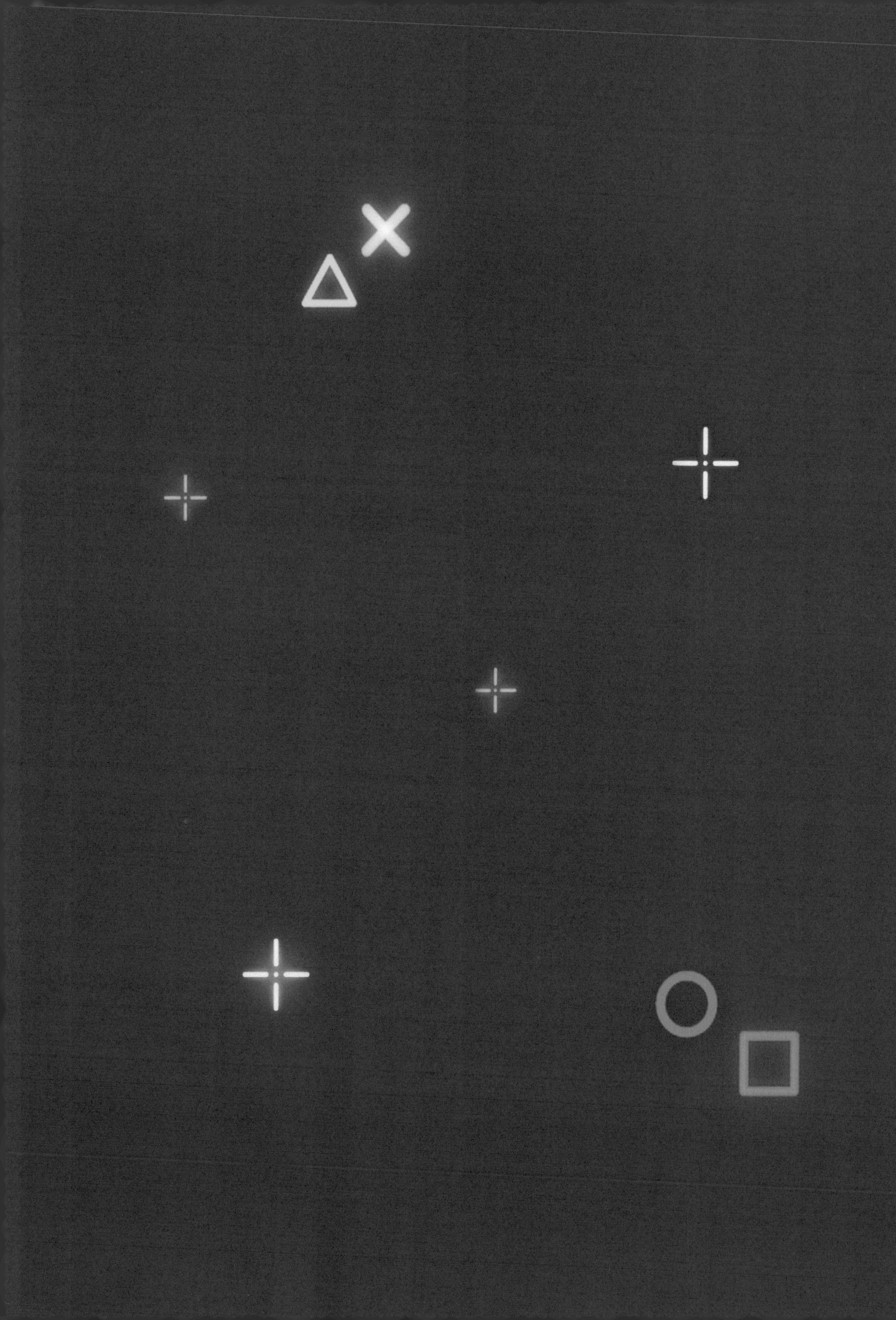

DANNY LOVES VIDEO GAMES

Based on the True Story of Danny Peña

By: MR. LUNA

Published in the United States by 2 Quality People, LLC.

For information about this title, other books, and/or special discounts for bulk purchases, contact the publisher:

2 Quality People
Books2QP@outlook.com

978-1-958490-06-8 (Ebook)
978-1-958490-07-5 (Ebook)
978-1-958490-04-4 (Hardback)
978-1-958490-05-1 (Paperback)

Edited by Mrs. Ani.

Printed in the United States of America.

DEDICATED TO

Godfree, aka el científico, the family is proud of you

When Danny was a kid,
he would spend all of his time playing at the arcades.
He really, really loved playing.
He would stay there all day!

Then, his grandma gifted him an Atari 2600,
and everything changed.

Instead of going to the arcade,
he would stay in his room playing Atari all day!
He was in love! He must've played video games for 23 hours a day.
Danny would play video games in the morning.
He would play video games in the afternoon.
He even played video games while everyone was sleeping.

One day, Danny's parents walked into his room,
and his father asked,
"What do you want to be when you grow up?"

“When I grow up, I’m going to work in the video game business,” said Danny. “You’ll see.”

A few years later, as technology evolved,
Danny received another gift.
This time it was a Nintendo game system.

Throughout the years,
Danny would always stay up to date with the newest gaming systems.

His passion for video games grew stronger as he got older, but his parents were very concerned about Danny's future.

"What are you going to do when school is over?" asked Danny's father. "Remember that playing video games doesn't pay the bills, son."

Danny understood what his father was trying to teach him, but his passion for video games grew stronger day by day.

As the years passed by,
Danny decided to try something new.
He was going to start a video game talk show.

GAMERTAG
RADIO

Danny was going to talk about all the latest and greatest video games,
and he was going to review them on this show.
He named the show "Gamertag Radio."

Danny teamed up with his little brother, and they immediately started practicing and recording the first episode.

GAMERTAG
RADIO

Once he felt comfortable, he took things to the next level.
He created the "Gamertag Radio Podcast."
His audience started growing from this online show,
and gamers from all over the world would listen to Danny.
He would inform the listeners about everything
that had to do with video games.

After a few years and a lot of hard work,
Danny was nominated for the Best Produced Podcast Award.
He felt super excited and honored
to be at the special Red Carpet event.

"Since I was a kid, I always knew what I wanted,
and I never gave up!" said Danny.

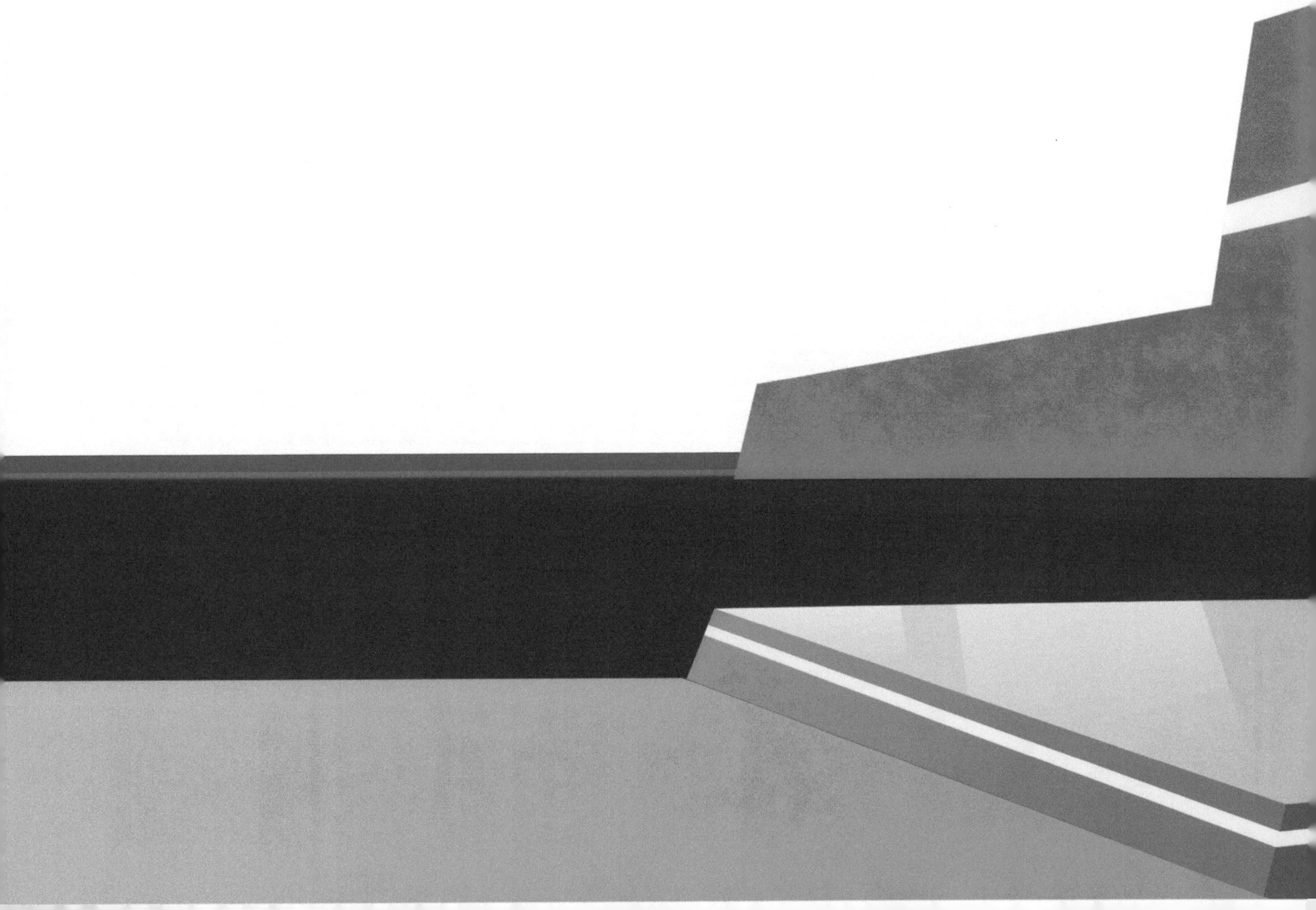

Keanu Reeves

Snoop Dogg

B-Real

Warren G

KRS ONE

Janina Gavankar

Danny Trejo

Giancarlo Esposito

Dawn Wells

After receiving his award,
Danny mentioned, "It has been a dream come true.
I've had the honor of interviewing several Hollywood stars
and some of my favorite artists."

"It wasn't easy for me to get here," said Danny.
"My hard work and consistency are finally paying off."
As he looked at the audience, he told them,
"Now I finally understand that old saying.
If you work doing what you love every day,
you will never work a day in your life."

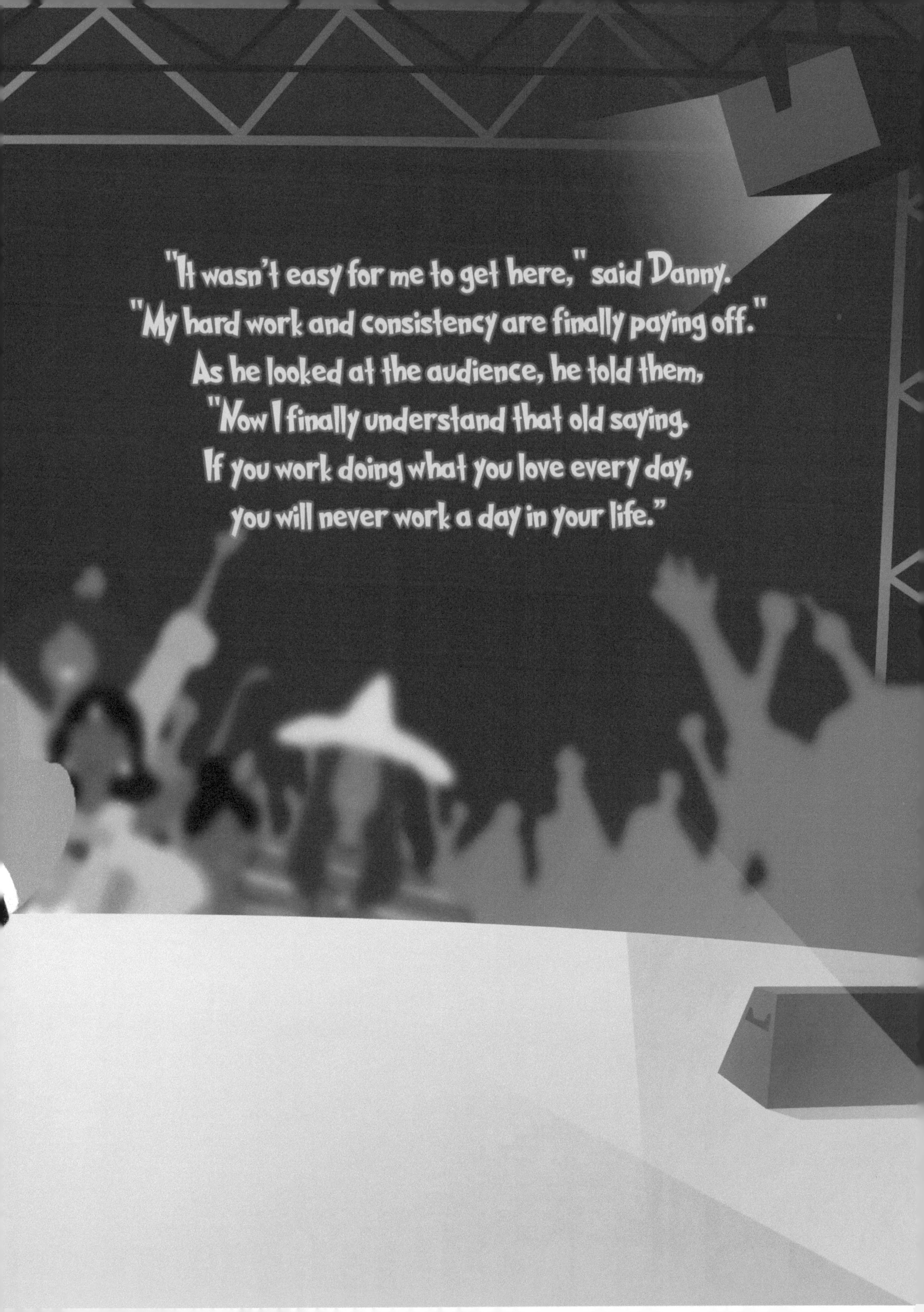

FUN FACTS ABOUT DANNY

*Gamertag Radio is the first gaming podcast to release 1,000 episodes.

*Danny is the first Latino to get inducted into the Podcast Hall of Fame.

*Danny's first film, "Gamertag Radio: A Podcast Story," won an award for Best Feature Film at the Super Geek Film Festival.

*While Danny was creating Gamertag Radio, he worked with many great TV networks such as Telemundo, Discovery Channel, Cheddar, CBS, and currently with G4.

Danny and his wife, Riana, in Times Square, NYC

CPSIA information can be obtained
at www.ICGtesting.com
Printed in the USA
LVHW071350080922
727700LV00023B/173

* 9 7 8 1 9 5 8 4 9 0 0 4 4 *